Learn With Animals

In the
Sea

By Laura Ottina
Adapted by Barbara Bakowski

Illustrated by
Sebastiano Ranchetti

WEEKLY READER®
PUBLISHING

Let's visit the ocean.
Let's go and explore,
From the foamy waves
To the sea's dark floor.

I am a dolphin.

I swim and I play.

I dive underwater

And leap in the spray.

5

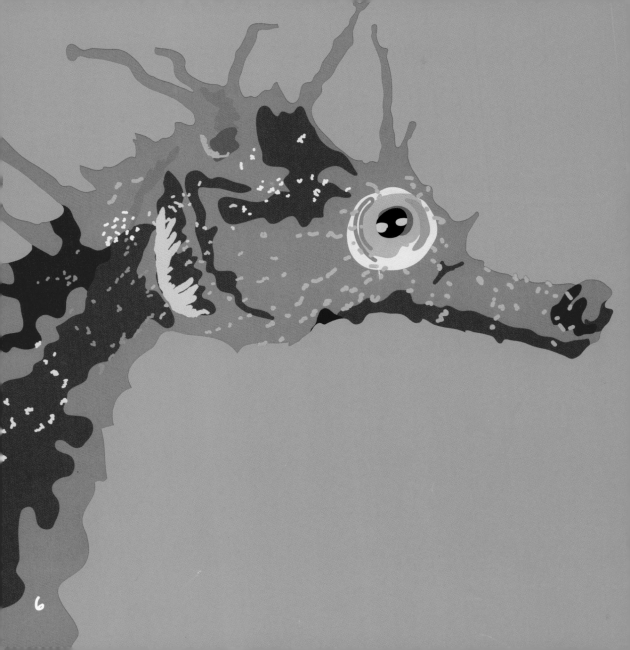

I am a seahorse
With a crown on my head.
In warm water I glide
Above the seabed.

I am a clown fish,
Bright orange and white.
Among the sea plants
I swim with delight.

9

I am a great white,
A shark with strong jaws
And rows of long teeth
As sharp as saws!

I am a jellyfish,
A curious thing
With no bones or brain
But, oh, what a sting!

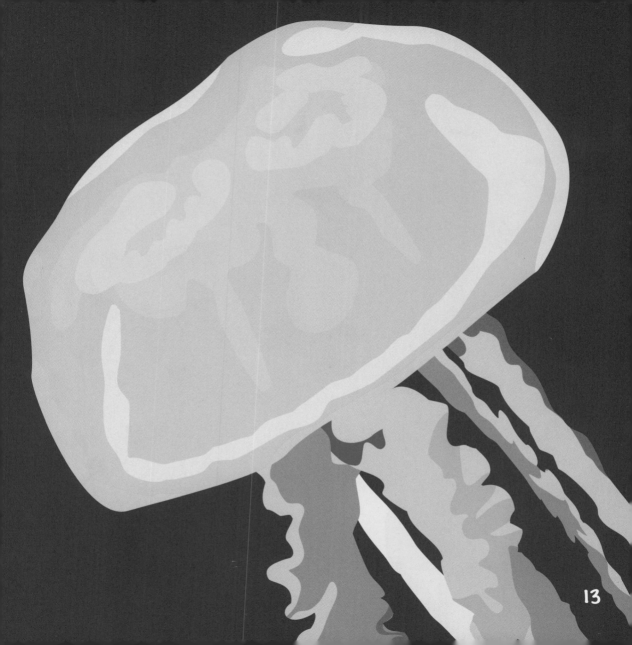

14

I am a porcupine fish,
Both clever and prickly.
When a big shark swims by,
I puff up so quickly!

I am a shrimp.
My shell I can shed.
When it gets too small,
I grow a big one instead.

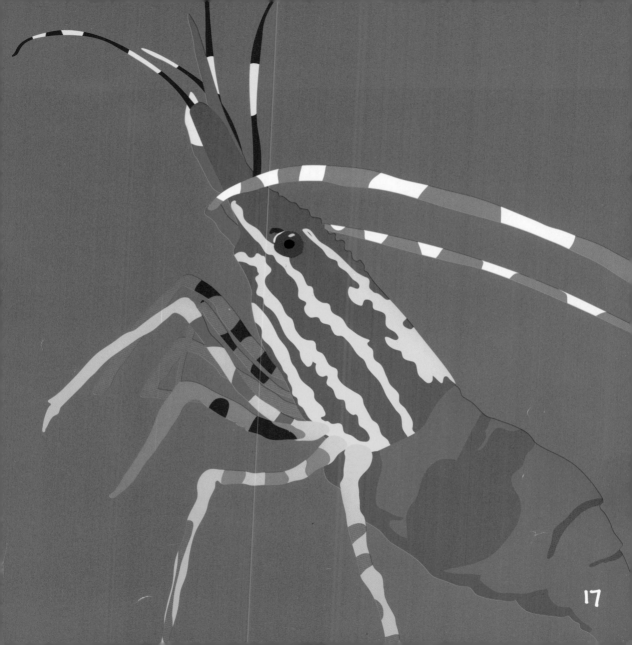

17

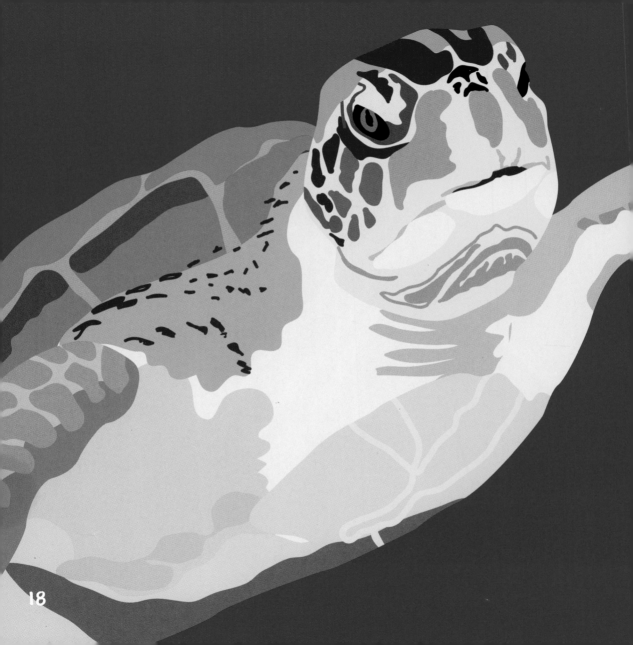

I am a green turtle.
On sea grass I feed.
With flippers like paddles
I swim with great speed.

I am an octopus.
From my garden I sneak,
Changing my color
To play hide-and-seek!

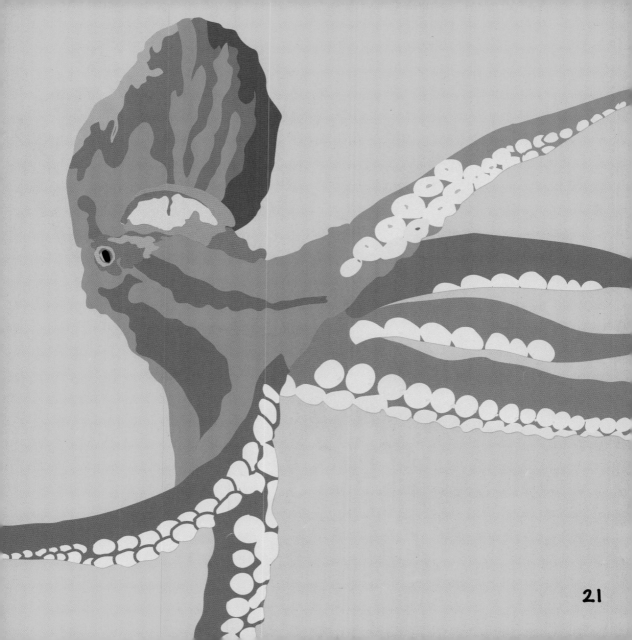

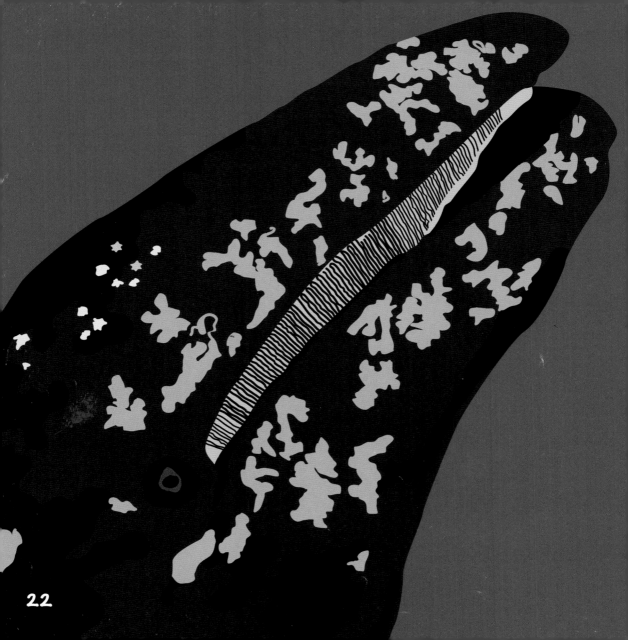

22

I am a gray whale,
With a mouth big and wide
That I fill with seawater
To trap fish inside.

Please visit our web site at **www.garethstevens.com**.
For a free catalog describing our list of high-quality books,
call 1-800-542-2595 (USA) or 1-800-387-3178 (Canada).
Our fax: 1-877-542-2596

Library of Congress Cataloging-in-Publication Data
Ottina, Laura.
      [Incontra gli animali nel mare. English]
      In the sea / by Laura Ottina ; adapted by Barbara Bakowski ;
illustrated by Sebastiano Ranchetti.
            p. cm. — (Learn with animals)
      ISBN-10: 1-4339-1914-1   ISBN-13: 978-1-4339-1914-5 (lib. bdg.)
      ISBN-10: 1-4339-2091-3   ISBN-13: 978-1-4339-2091-2 (softcover)
      1. Marine animals—Juvenile literature.   I. Bakowski, Barbara.   II. Ranchetti, Sebastiano, ill.
III. Title.
      QL122.2.O8813   2010
      591.77—dc22   2008052378

This North American edition first published in 2010 by
Weekly Reader® Books
An Imprint of Gareth Stevens Publishing
1 Reader's Digest Road
Pleasantville, NY 10570-7000 USA

Gareth Stevens Executive Managing Editor: Lisa M. Herrington
Gareth Stevens Senior Editor: Barbara Bakowski
Gareth Stevens Creative Director: Lisa Donovan
Gareth Stevens Designer: Jennifer Ryder-Talbot

Printed in the United States of America

1 2 3 4 5 6 7 8 9 12 11 10 09

Find out more about Laura Ottina and Sebastiano Ranchetti at **www.animalsincolor.com**.